Pilgrim

Pilgrim

Poems for the Journey

Mary Tarantini

RESOURCE *Publications* · Eugene, Oregon

PILGRIM
Poems for the Journey

Resource Publications
An Imprint of Wipf and Stock Publishers
199 W. 8th Ave., Suite 3
Eugene, OR 97401

www.wipfandstock.com

PAPERBACK ISBN: 978-1-6667-5305-9
HARDCOVER ISBN: 978-1-6667-5306-6
EBOOK ISBN: 978-1-6667-5307-3

09/02/22

"In Domino Confido" originally published in Bez & Co, online journal, April 2021

"Gira Sole" originally published in Bez & Co, online journal, July 2021

"Stubborn Is a Kind of Power" originally published in NJ Bards Poetry Review 2022

Dedicated to and in Memory of
Mr. Joseph Truitt
English Teacher Extraordinaire

Contents

Thank You God for Poetry

Thank you God for poetry
For lines molded, refined like afternoon tea

Thank you God for stanza and rhyme
For order and depth and beauty sublime

Thank you God for meaning and words
For truth so raw that it wrangles the nerves

Thank you God for voices that sow
Remembrances of lives lived long long ago

Thank you God as I put pen to paper
And offer these words as love's greatest labor

God Moved Into the Neighborhood

God moved into the neighborhood
I opened my front door
A surge of swallows swept down the street
And shook me to the core

I followed to the ocean shore
A dove with silver wings
Flew past me with a knowing smile
On her way to crown the King

A wave reached up and blessed the sky
And then returned to me
Enveloping my soul in bliss
Then flowed north with the sea

My feet sank deep into the sand
My spirit lifted free
A voice as lonely as the wind said—
Come and follow me

I Found It in an Old Wardrobe

I found it in an old wardrobe
Beneath a folded pile
Of woolen socks and cotton sheets
Was old and not in style
The color made me smile

Was deeper than the deepest hue
Of joy and fear and wonder
A sense of loss and déjà vu
A life lived full of summers

I picked it up and put it on
It was a perfect piece
There was no seam, no stitch, no flaw
No stain, no tear, no crease

Now I wear the love of Christ
All hours of the day
The folds of peace envelope me
Like night the Milky Way

For One Moment I Was With You

For one moment I was with you
An hour and a day
A rapture in the blood and bones
That takes the breath away

The sweetness overwhelmed me
Bliss became my norm
An intimation of a home
Our hearts have always borne

There is no sense, only silence
A beating of a kind
That fills the hollowed hearts of exiles
Seeking the Divine

Galileo

The first star of a billion years
Shines over the face of the deep
Watching through his prison window
Galileo—cries himself to sleep

He does not know that he is stardust
Such matter eludes his telescope
The impulse of all force and motion
The Father, Son, and Holy Ghost

Devotion anchors faith and heeds
All Knowledge is Truth and Holy
Galileo kneels and concedes
God redeems the meek and lowly

A Minor Life

To those who live a minor life
Appraising all interior spaces
Hiding out below the radar
Seeking all the lowly graces

Humility, a badge of honor
Hide it in your dresser drawer
Tailor habits, plain and gracious
Layer life in robes of sameness

In Domino Confido

"Some trust in chariots and some in horses"
Some seek to join the parade of immortals
Some parade wisdom through endless discourses
In Domino Confido

How do the angels guard and befriend?
A penny, a sign, from on high they descend?
The image of you in my sleep as I dreamt?
Deus amor est

God speaks to us in a gentle whisper
So heard Elijah after the wind and the fire
Respond in kind to this holy elixir
Amor vincit omnia

"When At Last Our Exile Here Is Ended"

I will see Your Face iridescent and splendid
And joy before now unfelt unheard
Stirs the ashes and dust of souls long interred

When at last the spell of time is broken
And seamless we are and never were nor will be
Rejoice—the perpetual Jubilee

When at last the voice of Cassandra is heeded
And Hera laughs last who cried most
"And the greatest of these is Love," She wrote

"When at last our exile here is ended"
And the river flows to the ends of the earth
We will travel across—on wings transplendent

Saint Therese

Saint Therese opened a door
And stepped into a world
Where vanity is draped in black
And hours retreat unheard
Where humility is all the rage
And a soul too small to dodge
Aches to caress the Eucharist—
On forbidden ground she trods—
Braid her hair with edelweiss
A life marked twice by sacrifice

Pauper Goddess

I ran the race
Was true and fair
Detractors gathered round
No unkind word nor selfish err
In wake of mine was found

Self-deprecation closed the gap
We galloped side by side
I sought and found my steadfast solace
In soup kitchens and shanty towns
Where lives the pauper goddess

Her white sari
And downward glance
Belied her fervent passion
To imitate and finish last
And seal love through devotion

I Prayed For Healing

I prayed for healing
Closed my eyes
And faced the rising East
A voice within, without, above
Promised no release

I prayed for safety
Free me from
The hate which loads the gun
Good luck with that, I heard quite clear
It's better if you run

What lies I've read my whole life through
Too numerous to count
My little words like grains of sand
Offered up in tears
Fell silently, one by one, from such careless hands

Stop squawking, child, all the noise
You raise has no true merit
Please read between the lines
Suffering and boundless grace
Is all you will inherit

She Knelt Before the Crucifix

She knelt before the crucifix
And all the world knelt too
Follow my example
Take heed I first loved you

The beads fell from her hands
Silence collapsed her ears
A thousand souls rushed in and jeered
Taunting her to tears

Why did you not expect
A cleansing to the bone
Press your face against the ground
Welcome your new home

Pilgrim

Pilgrim, where do you reside?
By the sea or mountainside?
Where is your forever home?
Anyplace your feet do roam?
Have you paid a price too high?
For your castle beneath the sky?
The view will take your breath away—
Or so the realtor will say.
Flags and loyalty count as loss.
What you gather you will someday toss.
Stranger or resident alien,
You are neither patriot nor citizen.
Have you slipped beyond this temporal world?
Are you on the altar with our Lord?

Lesson Learned

I held on tightly till my fingers
Warped from red to white
The object burst then showered down
Like fireworks at night
I searched the scant debris
Now scattered by my feet
As a baffled novice contemplates
The meaning of defeat
Like Lazarus, the lesson learned
Stung every ear that heard
To have and hold all that you treasure
Unto God's hands be transferred

Inside

I raised the cover, glanced inside
I was surprised to find
A slight and tattered object for which
All the world did pine

Negligible of capital
Neither gold nor silver shone
Yet many proffer life and limb
To haul said trifle home

I smiled slightly, closed the lid
Humanity must wait
Who am I to open wide
The straight and narrow gate?

Lighter Than Air

I remember the day you floated away
The grass stirred as a breeze sailed in
You lifted and hovered five feet above
Without a smile, surprise or hint of chagrin

A natural course of events you surmised
With no home or hearth or dollars or wife
Only a litany of prayers and good deeds
To show for your life

I wondered, amazed at this humble display
To empty oneself—finish lighter than air
Then drift with ease through the atmosphere
Without worry or loss or even fanfare

Devotion

A steady stream of force and motion
Surges past my wooden pew
Discharging what some call devotion
Time reels—then follows through

Devotion anchors faith and heeds
Not one can float adrift
Bury deep the tiny mustard seed
Your deeds, your song, your soul He sifts

May the oil in your lamp swell
Have you heard?
Emmanuel

This Music Is the Color White

This music is the color white
I followed where it led
Over mountains high and rivers wide
Where solitude is fed

Waiting in the dark of night
She called me by my name
She appeared in robes of milky white
Illumined from within

Senses coalesce in love
Love—is all she said
Music shimmered in her voice
Sound dangled by a thread

Her form—soft flowing curves of light
Her hands upon her breast
Ears to hear and hearts to see
God is as near as your next breath

She

She is the one who sings her song
When evening comes and day is done

She holds my hand on lonely days
When she sighs, the prairies sway

Crickets harken to her voice
To temper midnight's sleepless void

The wind, too, hears her overture
The mountains bow and welcome her

She counts the stars and names each one
And grants all pleas and dreams far flung

She shines her light on the forgotten
Sides with the lowly and downtrodden

Would you pretend to know her mind
And fathom life and death divine?

She decrees there is no slave nor free
All are one as all must be

How Does One Live?

Blessed Lady pray for us
Soothe our deep and darkest fears
Shine your light into the night
Whisper words we long to hear

Holy Mother cast your grace
On injured souls fueled by hate
Redeem the hearts of those who fear
Guide them through the narrow gate

Instruct us in the noble arts
Of justice, mercy, and love
March with those who hunger and thirst
Fill us with righteousness until our hearts burst

Holy Mother rescue those
Who walk each day under threat
To work, to school, to love, to play
Shield them like a bullet proof vest

Immaculate Woman, somber and sublime
A beacon for the ages
Stand among the grieving masses
Say the names of all the nameless

Blessed Lady the time is nigh
We feel it in our bones
Look as far as the eye can see
How does one live—who cannot breathe?

The Right Thing

The right thing to do
Is never a maze
It looks you straight in the face
And demands a full price
Refusing this grace
Is not my advice
Scruples emerge
Like an unwanted troll
Shifting the weight
From your mind to your soul
You will labor with ease
For this burden is light
The most it will ask
Is to lay down your life

Stonecatcher

Let me be a stonecatcher
The world is sore in need
Were I imprisoned for any deed
I pray remember me

Put down your stone the weight of which
Sinks deeply in your soul
Many summers sing to you
For me there are too few

When judgment rolls into my cell
Like rolling thunder clouds
Let blindness be its calling card
Mercy—its vanguard

Were you to catch the stone for me
The dawn would surely rise
On hillsides where the swaying grass
Meets the open skies

Holy Is

Holy is the Timberwolf
God painted you in gray
And gifted you a forest thick
With bark and shade and prey

Holy is the White Tailed Deer
Too numerous to count
Senses keen and bodies swift
Fly free and far without a sound

Humble is the Bumble Bee
Consorting in the fields
Friend of flower and all cuisine—
What power do you wield!

Mindful

I am mindful of the air I breathe
Of the wind on my cheek
From a cold morning breeze

I am mindful of the branches which sway
Outside my window
On a midsummer's day

I am mindful of the river's deep hue
And those who followed its course
In dugout canoes

I am mindful when I am alone with my thoughts
And memories profound
Dance a discordant waltz

I am mindful when I awake at dawn
From dreams descending in disarray
Like the Greek pantheon

I am mindful that I know nothing at all
We construct our tomorrows
Like a load bearing wall

Rather I float down a river
And—immersed in cool currents—
I laugh and I linger

The Mystery

The majesty of silence is this
A pebble on the road
The warmth below the ground in which
A seed is newly sown

The depths of coldness, dark and deep
When waters close above
That which sinks and disappears
A stone, a word, a love

The mystery of silence is this
The early morning rising mist
The letting go of self
Into one all colors melt

Lightning Bugs

Lightning bugs by far exceed
All diamonds, gold, and bling
To watch in silence as they flicker—
Vespers for a king

Words Release

Words release their darts and miss
More often than a novice
Dreams coerce the truth and then
Shower morning light upon us

My Home

My home is in the words I write
My bed the comfort of their rhyme
Syllables are every step I climb
Meaning—a lamp—iridescent by design

In Silence

In silence the earth renews itself
Listen—the dew grows and forms
Upon the tips of blades of grass
A daily, joyful, holy Mass

Stubborn Is a Kind of Power

Stubborn is a kind of power
You see it everywhere
Many miss the brief encounters
Sometimes they catch me unaware

I saw it in a patch of snow
One sunny winter day
A sea of green usurped its borders
Yet by night was held at bay

My favorite is the blue eggshell
Tiny—broken—below a tree
Wings stretched new upon a bough
Life escapes its own debris

Truth and Beauty

I was promised truth and beauty
Then I spoke the words
That, in my heart, leapt and shimmered
Yet never was I heard

They pushed me into a tunnel and said
Find and follow your heart
Darkness like an oil slick spread
No depth, no breadth, no chart

Step after step, the walls they glimmered
As my beauty passed on by
Within my corporeal form—
A luminous liquid glowed—
From which no truth could hide

Blackbird

Blackbird in a green field
You are not afraid
The worst that can happen is not the worst
Only mayhem is man made

Blackbird with a silver eye
There are fires and floods and lies
Somewhere, below the stars,
There is room for compromise

Blackbird in a field of green
O, stretch your wings, your one true talent
Fly across that finish line
Hungry, bruised, and gallant

Black as night and green as life
To dream is the sacrificial rite

I Asked

I asked and waited with bated breath
I sought and naught revealed
I knocked and fell into the open sea
Here I am, send me!

No voice replied—that I could hear
No whisper, no breath, no sigh—
My feet slipped through a crevice in time
Into a world divine

Now I roam the valley deep
And sample the morning mist
All that is and nothing else rises
From a silence profound and timeless

Silence speaks in amber resin
Transparent, golden, eternal pause
In her presence sing a new song
Rivaling the purple dawn!

I Saw You

I saw you walking
On the inside of the edge
Mourning each step while letting go
What do you know that I don't know?

I saw you stalking
The moon last night
Peering through glass like Galileo
Do you see Heaven in the misty glow?

I heard you praying
Without words, psalms or beads
Folding blue into purple into indigo
Surrendering beneath the weeping willow

I saw you smiling
As you came up for air
Planting your feet in the rolling meadow
Unfolding like the Rose of Jericho

When Nature Dreams

When nature dreams the mountains rise
And crumble in one day
The bluebird sings a symphony
In Swedish and Françias

Flowers bloom and fade and bloom
And fade for hours and hours—
The unremitting play of life
Staged in brief encounters

Oceans spill their treasures ashore—
Golden trident and glistening mermaids
Poseidon, with one scoop, retrieves
His priceless runaways

Dreams are fancy, dreams are truth
Dreams purge and dreams expire
Yet what nature entertains
Will set the world afire!

Silence

Wrap me up in the past
Then spin me free of time and space
Inspiration invades my senses
Rising from the commonplace

While I wait for random praise
And cast my pearls upon the floor
Oceans beckon, landscapes listen
Silence is a higher chore

Silence dictates in absentia
Sovereign, Empress, Matron, Queen
Follow her through lowly places
Lucky those her favors glean

Words

I wish that you had lived
To see how your words swell
And fill the hearts of dreamers far
And soothe the ear with rhyming knell

You place your words upon a page
Like a minuet flits across the stage

Is life too fine to touch?
Dreams too fine to dream?
Let loose the soul of all your words
Then hide away to the extreme

You place your words just out of reach
Like dreams dispel at break of sleep

A verse can charm the heavy heart
Like words proposed and soon forgotten
Tell a truth then fling it far
Beyond the rings of Saturn

I Wrote a Letter

I wrote a letter to my heart
I asked her for a sign
Were you the one I'm waiting for?
She wrote back—are you blind?
The stars aligned the day we met
Two sparrows circled round
Our ancestors cast their lots
And bid us wear the crown
Of joyfulness and sadness
That flows from consecrated love
Like blue upon a canvass

Superpower

If I am honest to a T
And dot my i's in ink
Can I exchange said beauty for truth
A flower for a candlestick
To commemorate the holy hour
I placed my heart upon my sleeve
And offered you my superpower—
A comrade to believe

I Love You Best

I love you best in wintertime
When the moon is high in the dark blue sky
And every thought I have of you
Floats free and far and feels brand new

I love the wind and the chill in the air
I love the warmth beneath the blanket we share
The evening is quiet and simple and long
And hours drift in the dark between the rooms until dawn

Love gathers like snow upon a windowsill
A soft presence peering into our souls
Dismissing the old, sweeping cobwebs away—
Dispersing joy like a cabaret

Gira Sole

Turn to the sun, magnificent flower
Show us all the way
There is no shame in primal power
There is no shame in grand display

Docile habits draw us inward
Yellow is thy flame
In my ear you dared to whisper
Summer is your name

Howling wind nor sudden downpour
Dissuade you from your steadfast mission
Stand in thrall—divest—adore
Impetuous devotion

One Early Summer Eve

You alighted on my shoulder
One early summer eve
Butterfly of significance
Creature of motifs

Your court you held with open wings
Meeting my eye with ease
Butterfly of prerogative
Master of prestige

The moment lasted just long enough
Then you must be on your way
Butterfly of destiny
Ambassador of faraway

The lowly on the food chain
Journey a thousand miles
Butterfly of humility
Sister to the skies

Dreams

I dreamed about you last night
I dreamed you were alive
You walked into the room—you said
Here—the rules do not apply

When sorrow bruises an open wound
And longing cuts deep and wide
Permission is hereby granted
To step across the great divide

Just who am I to thank?
He Who giveth and taketh away?
You smile gently—*Do not resist*
A humble soul gives sway

Jacob wrestled—and prevailed—
Dreams sustain the cosmic core
I open my eyes as morning breaks
All is as was before

As I Walked Down By the River

As I walked down by the river
There appeared to me to be
A dream upon the water
Floating east toward the sea

I left it there many years ago
When sirens beckoned to other shores
The day was all I understood
For endless were the open doors

Why it drifted, carefree and slow
I wondered as I rested
Upon the bank of moss and clover
As evening approached, sweet and sober

I watched the dream follow its course
Then continued on my way—
Dispatching all remorse

Enkidu

There's immortality they say
In a brushstroke, in a pen
So I offer the gods a blank page
To be with you again

The eternal quest of Gilgamesh
Spun from twines of grief
Ends at the tomb of man's fair share
Unraveling as he weeps

If I could I would
Fill the Holy Grail, sumptuous and sweet
Pluck halos from the heads of saints
And lay them tenfold at your feet

Gospel or legend
It's really quite extraordinary
The lengths one will travel for a friend

Inherit the Earth

We sidle up to greatness
Fame is a nom de plume
While the legions of lowly and nameless
Travel onward in ashen costumes

The garb of dreary simplicity
Somber hues of dry wood and dry hearth
A vast column of squalid humanity
Marches forward to inherit the earth

Blink once and the masses have gathered
Twice and the planet will sway
What you thought was forsaken and scattered
Rises up and seizes the day

Imperfection

I'm not too young to misinterpret
Nor too old for stage direction
The world appears to me annoyed
At my slightest imperfection

The unfettered and the unsung
Conversate in whispers
They glide among the tallest trees
And drink from the big dipper

They keep no tally
But to note how early rise the sun
How many hours is the day
How many tales homespun

Who reaches down to touch the sky
Has no penchant to complain
Perfection is an afterthought
When dancing in the rain

Fool's Gold

She is the sun, she is the moon
She is the pawn, Pandora
The stars reflect her radiance
She directs the rain and thunder

Redemption courses through her blood
The crow is her protector
The blackbird and the raven
Spiral round her golden scepter

Who would be her lover?
She cradles her tattered heart in the night
All, yet none, will call her Mother
Her sorrow is her heart's delight

Her true love did relinquish her—
A gesture to her eternal maidenhood
Though she is strong and tall and bold
There she remains—his fool's gold

Recovery Road

I like you on these temperate days
As we travel down Recovery Road
I don't mind when you stop halfway
And drop a bundle to lighten your load
It's all right, you say then pick up the pace
There are no burdens that can't be replaced

I like this path that we venture on
I like the way that you pull me along
There are no pitfalls or detour signs
We watch the road not what lies beyond
The milestones may be far between
But gratitude flows leisurely downstream

Bluebird

The bluebird sings a silent song
To hear her some do leap and dance
While others throw their coins away
On games of luck and whims of chance

Some hear the song a summer night
When crickets trill and lovers sigh
But those are only future echoes
Of grief unbound and dreams awry

The song is tranquil, brazen, noble
At times a note off key
Scoops plunder from a buried treasure
Then begins the Jubilee—

I keep my bluebird on a shelf
To hear the strains, richly lyrical
For when they chance to flow and resound
From every daily ritual

Loneliness Is an Indiscretion

I tuck the hours away in a drawer
And watch the minutes pass in dwindling procession
To those with ribbons, parades, and bling galore
Loneliness is an indiscretion

A mantra for the tender-footed
"To be or not"—crack open the door
Solitude swells as hindsight enters
Measuring the day in shadows across the floor

I should have embraced each and every attachment
Typed in yea instead of nay then perhaps—
The question boomerangs without an answer
How to reconcile a life elapsed?

Letting Go

The saddest thought I ever had
Is buried deep inside
Below the silent sands of grief
A million oceans wide

I thought that in the days to come
A tidal wave full force
Would set you down right at my feet
A miracle of sorts

Horizons are a distant gamble
Mirages abound
Truth is my confessor
Brutal and profound

Sadness I can swallow
Self-pity entertain
But letting go the dream of you
Will drive me pure insane

My Bad

You trespass in my head
My bad, I let you in
A skip and a jump to my heart
The reason I never win

The littlest violin plays my tune
Pulls me in every time
I'd rather sink than swim a mile
Wanting you ain't such a crime

You left a piece of you in me
Such a heartless game of guile
It wanders randomly between soul and marrow
Think I'll wait here for awhile

If I Take You Back Again

If I take you back again I'd be
A child
Who counts 1, 2, 3

If I take you back again I'd feel
Exhilaration
Having sealed the deal

If I take you back again I'd spy
For clues
In every corner of your eyes

I'd own your smile for a while
The most delicious kisses, forever potent,
Would cost me my last token

Love is a long haul
For you
An order too tall

If I take you back again I'd be
The definition of insanity

This Rhyme

I wish my life were like this rhyme
Contrived and eloquent
My heart would soar to heights sublime
And never feel desolate

Timed and rehearsed, we'd parley in verse
I love you and you love me
I would have you back in my arms again
Before the cadence hit stanza three

A thought once uttered floats adrift
The gesture is what you confess
We measure actions, silent and swift
Words are hollow and meaningless

I Love You Are Three Words

I love you are three words that taste
Like bubble gum when said in haste
Compare me to a traveling show
Pedaling cures for all that ails
Masking the truth in a million details

Parade me out for all to see
Time the promises to a tee
I left my yardstick when you called
And fell too hard, too long, too deep
Assail me not if I sold myself cheap

Who can discern the heart's recess?
Just walk one mile, more or less
Slip on my sandals, warm and worn
Remember selflessness is never passé
Fling sweet sentiments along the way

Open Window

Years pressed deep down under the thumb
I crawl out slowly hand against the sun
Twenty years internment
Is enough for anyone

The fumes of my drunk captor
Held me by the throat
I lost my ears, my eyes, my soul, my voice
Each second survived became my drink of choice

Such a pittance is no reward
Living one hour at a time
So I leap through to tomorrow
My song my words my saving rhyme

Grab my hand why don't you follow
Forgive, forget and gather round
The open window whoops and hollers
I'll race you to that sound

I Am Your Past

I am your past come face to face
Be forewarned and sit astride
All you thought you could erase
Sloshes back in with the tide

I am asking for this dance
Time's a nut you cannot crack
Specters appear as if by chance
What's forgotten is what you lack

I have come in with you to dine
Like sacraments, I fill each space
With a sweet or bitter wine

Humility

Kings are an endangered species
Time—has taken its toll
Pageantry like ruby slippers
Clings to the wearer's soul
Better, don a coarse brown tunic
Walk barefoot down the road
Sport humility in grandest fashion
Like the emperor's new clothes

A Lost Crusade

And so the earth is scorched with grief
A thousand jump ropes at your feet
The reaper stakes his battleground
The catcher in the rye cries out

Heed him now before you fade
Lest every dream a lost crusade

Rapunzel

Rapunzel, let down your hair
Your patience is wearing thin
The longer you stare out the window
Rehearsing "Oh, where have you been?"
The louder the chorus will chant
And play on their tiny violins

Gather your skirt, run down the stairs
There is a door, you know
The key was fashioned long ago
(And to you we duly bestow)
By those who well know their own worth
In Heaven and here down on earth

Betta Bride

Something tells me I am more
A stirring in my soul
A quiet recognition
And my heart begins to roll

You ask me for a lifetime
Is it mine to give?
The scorn and straps of ages past
Held me down in the abyss

I climb despite the veil and harness
And touch the midnight dome
Glass is but a handy mirror
Reflecting the rising dawn

You are kind and generous
I will be your betta bride
But, my love, keep your distance
Watch me swim against the tide

She Runs

How long will she run?
Go—gushes through her veins
Not for fear or profit or circumstance
Save to establish her domain

She runs to purify the perfect
Of all its trivial acquisitions
To shame the pang of dissatisfaction
And banish expectation

How far will she run?
Longevity is a gift
A gracious life nails the center in place
And never will she drift

She runs without a number
Without apology or plume
Speed—a liability
Sweat—the sweetest perfume

Queen of Domesticity

She was queen of pitter patter
Queen of hugs and all that matters
Of grocery carts and dying eggs
Of picture frames and hide-n-seek games

Queen of tummy aches and tired laughter
Pushing swings and running after
Of stretch marks and elasticity
She was queen of domesticity

She labored two jobs to fill the coffers
She was queen of loose change and too few dollars
Of torn window screens and leaky faucets
Surreptitiously the subject of neighborhood gossip

Queen of running late and early hours
Sleepless nights and imaginary powers
To retrieve wayward dreams from beyond
With a simple wave of her magic wand

She dreamed of high heels and short black dresses
Yet returned each day to ungodly messes
For she was queen of unsung songs
Queen of all that could go wrong

Once she dreamed of white gowns and throwing rice
Yet being alone so long she never learned to play nice
So she politely declined his offer of a ring
For what it's worth she dreamed of being king

Karma

Karma does not distinguish
Chance must step aside
Go ahead and spread that anguish
All you dread will soon collide

Give away your only dollar
Consider the Samaritan
Choose charity over power
Even history will chime in

Karma levels the playing field
Rejoice or rue the day
She will always have her say

The Time It Takes

The time it takes to find oneself
A lifetime, more or less
Beyond the windswept landscape
Assemble the base and dispossessed

I would have arrived much earlier
But for my carelessness
I never heard the bell that tolls
Such was my negligence

Socrates conjectured
Who knew not what he knew
I thought I saw and understood all
But the sky is only the shadow of blue

Through The Looking Glass

I hung a mirror on the wall in my bedroom
Almost imperceptibly everything changed
A new room emerged
Reflected through a disc of self-discovery
Drawing attention to itself
Suggesting
A world beyond
A dare—
Slip through
To the other side
Complacent bed and bureau, closet and lamp
Watch silently
The impromptu shift
Of a new perspective

Kaleidoscope

I carefully adhere to rules
Predict me like the evening tides
Call me faithful
Call me rude
Never look me in the eyes

I check the lights
I check the stove
Locking every door knob twice
My sanity rests upon
Remembering the words to every song

I see you clearly through my kaleidoscope
Each color is a key
There's order in disorder
Symmetry in the smallest speck
A treasure in a quarter

Turn the lens on me
Be amazed and downright humbled
Toss your hat into the ring
Life's a strange and wonderful gamble

My Love for You

My love for you is like the tide
Of oceans blue and deep and wide
Of whirlpools formed in placid lakes
When dreams spin free before I wake

Love is neither free nor sold
I held it in my hand but thrice
Then laid it down upon the sand
Perfecting love in sacrifice

I did not know that perfect love
Imprints your memory into my skin
And courses through my veins until
Your heart beats once again within

Were I once more asked to laugh, to cry
To be forever bound and tied
To watch youth erupt into young men
My love for you would gladly assent
Over and over and over again

I Love You More

When in my arms you reach beyond me
Then sing your song like a troubadour
That doesn't mean I love you less
I love you more

When in your youth you fight and falter
And scorn my voice, my words, my offer
That doesn't mean I love you less
I love you more

When seeking truth births pain, not bliss
And my presence you all but ignore
That doesn't mean I love you less
I love you more

When I am free, my exile over
And leave this world for one obscure
That doesn't mean I love you less
I love you more

When in your memory I cease to enter
And the waves wash my name from the shore
That doesn't mean my hour has ended
My love endures

www.ingramcontent.com/pod-product-compliance
Lightning Source LLC
Chambersburg PA
CBHW060420050426
42449CB00009B/2050